Contents

Differentiation of topics for 3 levels of ability

To differentiate the learning activities, the games have been colour coded according to the amount of Spanish words that appear in the games. "**verde**" is for the lower ability group, "**amarillo**" is for the middle ability group, and "**rojo**" is for the higher ability group. Ideally photocopy the mini cards onto card. The board games look nice on A4 or A3.

	verde	amarillo	rojo
Drinks	una Coca-Cola una limonada un zumo agua	una Coca-Cola una limonada un agua mineral un zumo de naranja un té un café	una Coca-Cola un té una limonada un café un agua mineral una leche un zumo de naranja una Coca-Cola light un batido de chocolate
Greetings	Hola Adiós por favor gracias	Hola sí Adiós no por favor gracias Buenos días Buenas tardes	Hola sí Adiós no por favor Buenas noches gracias Hasta luego Buenos días lo siento Buenas tardes de nada
Pet animals	un gato un perro un pez una serpiente	un gato un perro un pez una serpiente un conejo un caballo	un gato un pájaro un perro una tortuga un pez un ratón una serpiente un concjo un caballo
Clothes	un abrigo un jersey una camiseta unos vaqueros	un abrigo un jersey una camiseta unos vaqueros una falda unos pantalones cortos	un abrigo un vestido un jersey unos pantalones una camiseta una gorra unos vaqueros una falda unos pantalones cortos
Transport	el tren el autobús el barco el coche	el tren el autobús el barco el coche la bicicleta el avión	el tren la moto el autobús la barca el barco el cohete el coche la bicicleta el avión
Weather	Hace calor Hace frío Hace sol Llueve	Hace calor Hace frío Hace sol Llueve Hace buen tiempo Hace mal tiempo	Hace calor nieva Hace frío hay tormenta Hace sol está nublado Llueve Hace buen tiempo Hace mal tiempo

1

una Coca-Cola

una limonada

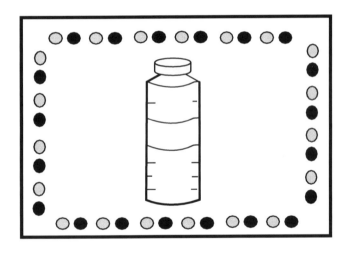

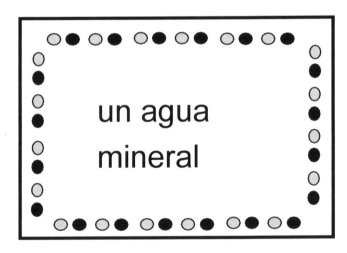

un agua
mineral

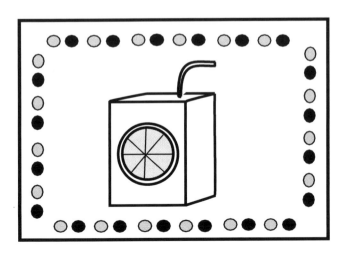

un zumo
de naranja

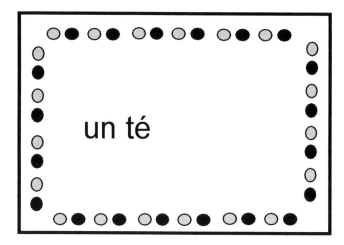

un té

un café

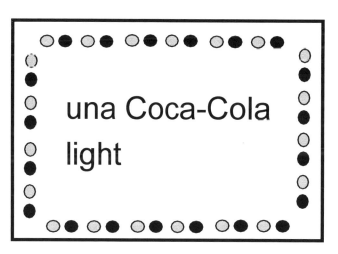

una Coca-Cola
light

una leche

Can I say 4 drinks in Spanish?

Start at "comienza aquí", roll the dice and count that number of squares.
Say the drink you land on in Spanish. To win, arrive first at "¡Has ganado!"

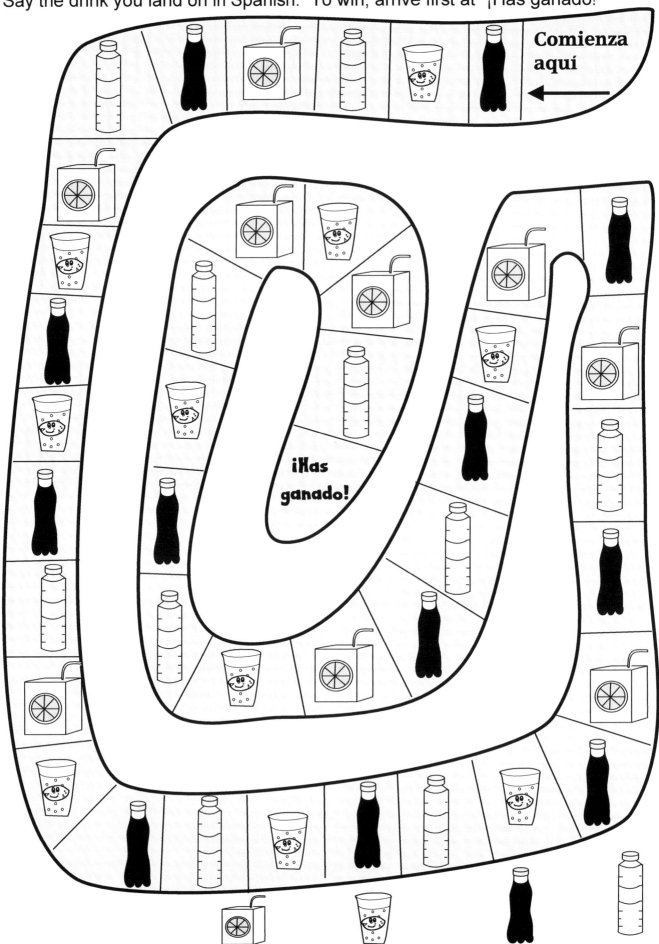

Comienza aquí

¡Has ganado!

un zumo   una limonada   una Coca-Cola   agua

4

Can I say 4 drinks in Spanish? - Pupil A

Each pupil cuts out a set of dominoes by cutting along the dotted lines.
Take turns to put a card down by matching a word to a picture or vice versa.
If you cannot match a card, miss a turn. The winner is the person to either
use all their cards, or use as many cards as possible.

Each pupil cuts out a set of dominoes by cutting along the dotted lines.
Take turns to put a card down by matching a word to a picture or vice versa.
If you cannot match a card, miss a turn. The winner is the person to either
use all their cards, or use as many cards as possible.

Can I say six drinks in Spanish?

Start at "comienza aquí", roll the dice and count that number of squares.
Say the drink you land on in Spanish. To win, arrive first at "¡Has ganado!"

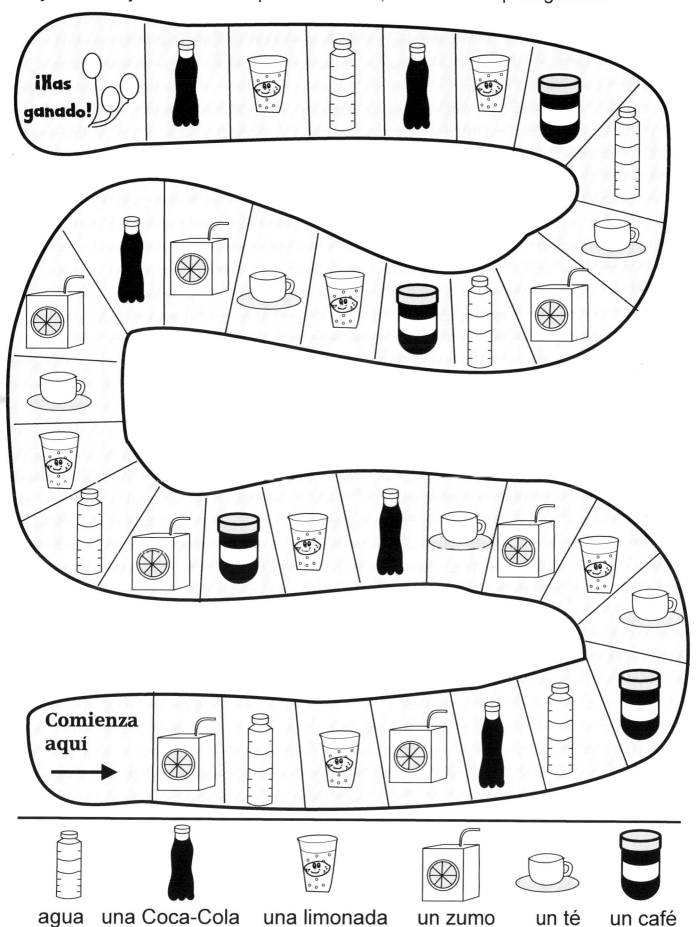

agua   una Coca-Cola   una limonada   un zumo   un té   un café

7

Can I say six drinks in Spanish?

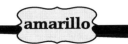

Each person / team needs 5 coloured counters or cubes of one colour (or a set of noughts or a set of crosses). Say the Spanish word for the drink or essential word as you cover it with your counter.
To win you have to get 3 in a row (vertically, horizontally or diagonally).

un agua   una Coca-Cola   una limonada   un zumo   un té   un café

Hola = Hello   por favor = please   gracias = thank you

Can I say 9 drinks in Spanish?

Start at "comienza aquí", roll the dice and count that number of squares.
Say the drink you land on in Spanish. To win, arrive first at "¡Has ganado!"

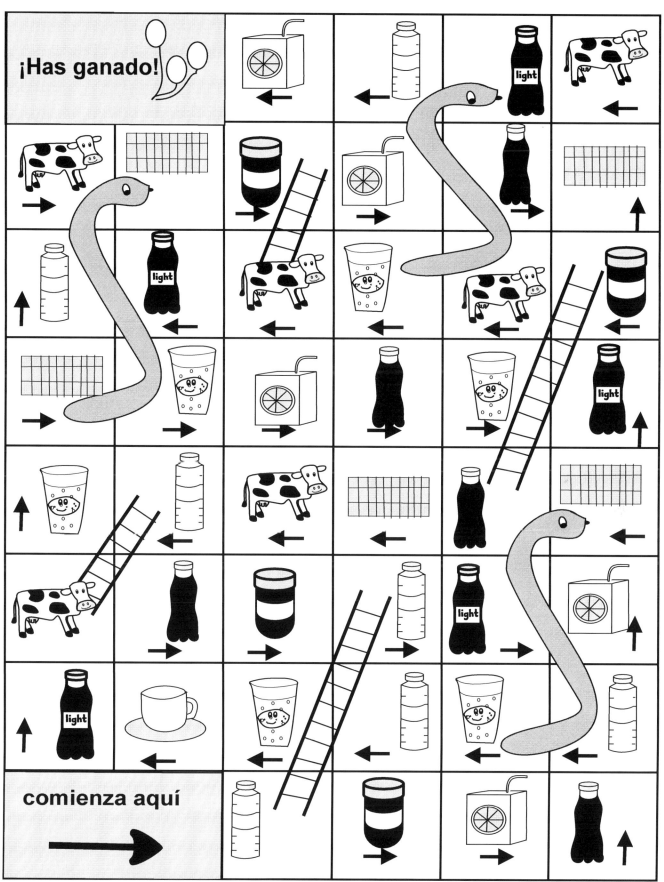

agua una Coca-Cola una limonada una Coca-Cola light

un zumo un té un café un batido de chocolate una leche

9

Can I say 9 drinks in Spanish?

Each person / team needs 5 coloured counters or cubes of one colour (or a set of noughts or a set of crosses). Say the Spanish word for the drink as you cover it with your counter.
To win you have to get 3 in a row (vertically, horizontally or diagonally).

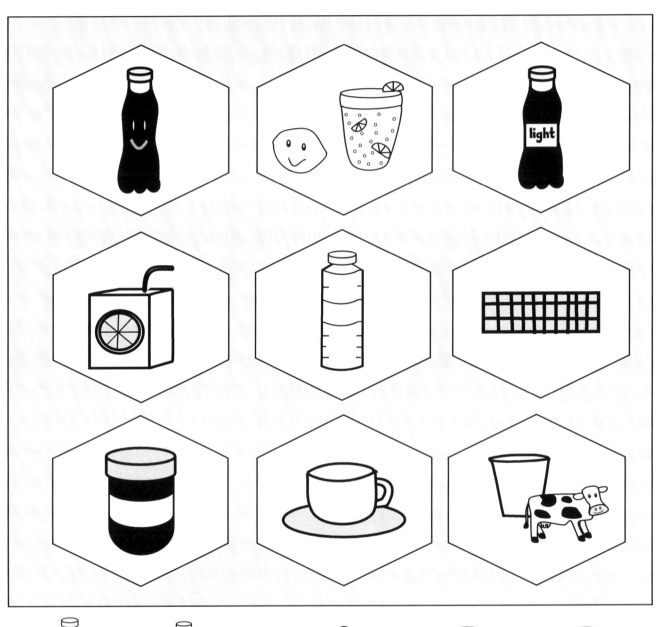

agua

una Coca-Cola

una limonada

un zumo

una Coca-Cola light

un té

un café

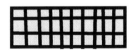
un batido de chocolate

una leche

10

Can I say 9 drinks in Spanish?

Roll two dice and find the **co-ordinate** by counting along the bottom for the first dice, and up the side for the second dice. Say the drink in Spanish for the co-ordinate to get a point, e.g. 3, 2 = una Coca-Cola light. The winner is the person or team who gets the most points.

agua   una Coca-Cola   una limonada   un zumo   una Coca-Cola light

un té   un café   un batido de chocolate   una leche

11

Hola

Hello

Adiós

Good bye

por favor

please

gracias

thank you

sí

yes

no

no

Buenos días

Good morning

Buenas tardes

Good afternoon

13

Buenas noches

Good night

Lo siento

I'm sorry

De nada

Don't mention it

Hasta luego

See you

Can I say 4 useful phrases in Spanish?

Start at "comienza aquí", roll the dice and count that number of squares.
Say the phrase you land on in Spanish. To win, arrive first at "¡Has ganado!"

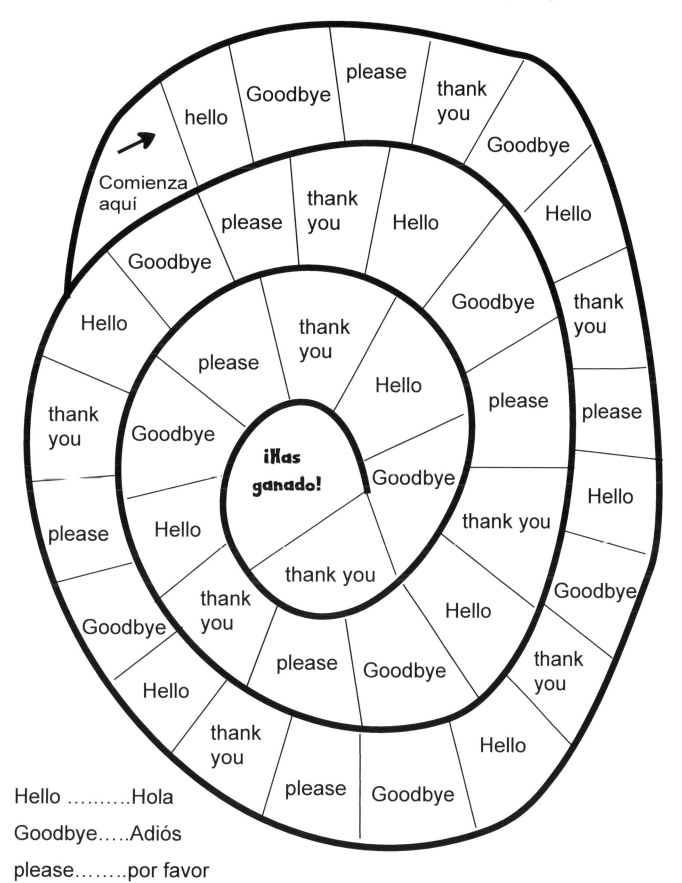

Hello ……….Hola

Goodbye…..Adiós

please……..por favor

thank you….gracias

Can I say 4 useful phrases in Spanish?

Each person / team needs 10 coloured counters or cubes of one colour.

Say the Spanish word for the phrase as you place your counter or cube.
To win you have to get 4 in a row (vertically, horizontally or diagonally).

Goodbye	please	Hello	thank you
Hello	Goodbye	thank you	please
thank you	Hello	Goodbye	Hello
please	thank you	please	thank you
Goodbye	please	Hello	Goodbye

Hello ……….Hola   Goodbye…..Adiós

please……..por favor   thank you….gracias

16

Can I say 8 useful phrases in Spanish?

Start at "comienza aquí", roll the dice and count that number of squares.
Say the phrase you land on in Spanish. To win, arrive first at "¡Has ganado!"

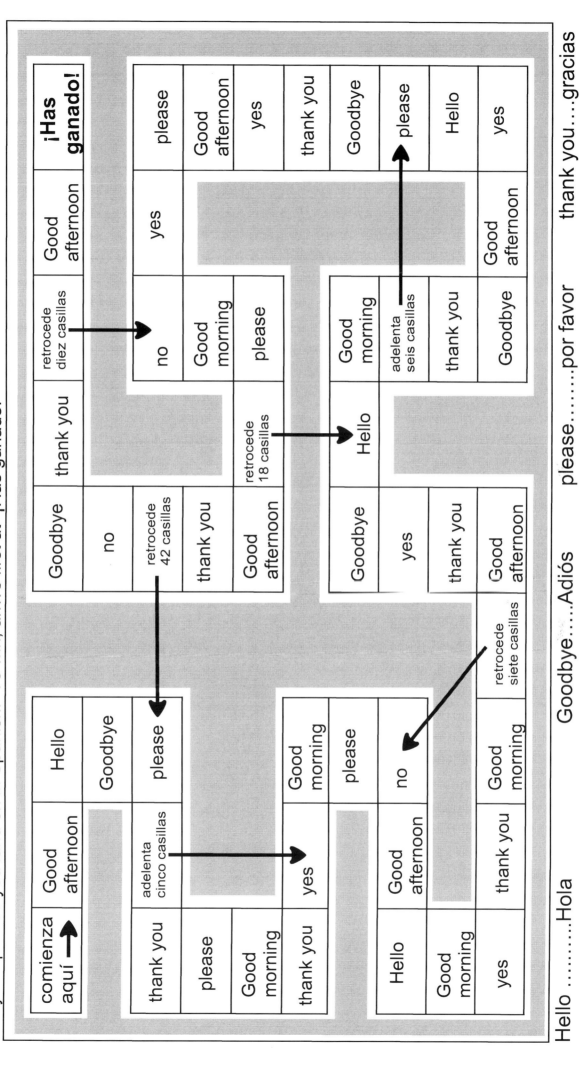

Hello ....Hola   Goodbye.....Adiós   please.......por favor   thank you....gracias

Good morning.......Buenos días   Good afternoon .....Buenas tardes   sí......yes   no......no

Each pupil cuts out a set of **dominoes** by cutting along the dotted lines. Take turns to put a card down by matching a Spanish phrase to an English phrase. If you cannot match a card, miss a turn. The winner is the person to either use all their cards, or use as many cards as possible.

sí	Good morning

por favor	Hello

no	Good afternoon

Adiós	no

Buenos días	yes

Hola	thank you

Buenas tardes	please

gracias	Good bye

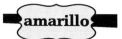

ach pupil cuts out a set of **dominoes** by cutting along the dotted lines.
ake turns to put a card down by matching a Spanish phrase to an English
hrase. If you cannot match a card, miss a turn. The winner is the person
either use all their cards, or use as many cards as possible.

Buenos días	please

Adiós	no

Hola	yes

Buenas tardes	Good bye

por favor	Hello

no	thank you

sí	Good morning

gracias	Good afternoon

Can I say 12 useful phrases in Spanish?

Start at "comienza aquí", roll the dice and count that number of squares.
Say the phrase you land on in Spanish. To win, arrive first at "¡Has ganado!"

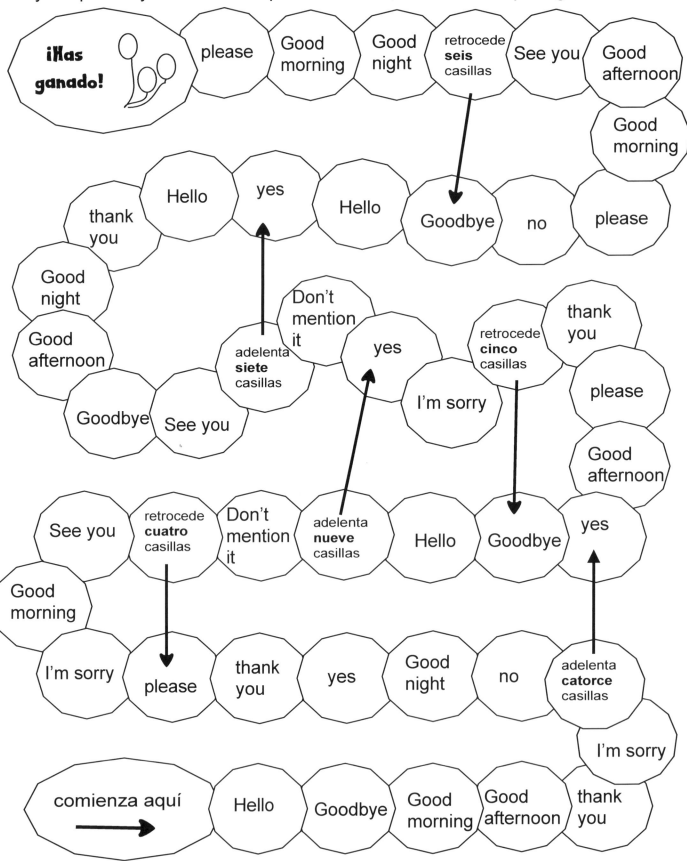

Hello ….…..Hola   Goodbye.….Adiós   please……..por favor   thank you….gracias

Good morning…..Buenos días   Good afternoon ….Buenas tardes   Good night…..Buenas noches

sí…….yes   no…….no   See you…..Hasta luego   I'm sorry….lo siento   Don't mention it …De nada

Each person / team needs 5 coloured counters or cubes of one colour (or a set of noughts or a set of crosses).

Say what the Spanish word means in English as you place your counter. To win you have to get 3 in a row (vertically, horizontally or diagonally).

Hola	**no**	**Adiós**
por favor	**sí**	**gracias**
Buenos días	**Buenos tardes**	**Buenas noches**

Hello ………Hola	Goodbye…..Adiós	please…….por favor
Good morning…….Buenos días	thank you….gracias	
Good afternoon ……Buenas tardes	yes…….sí	
Good night…………..Buenas noches	no……..no	

un gato

un perro

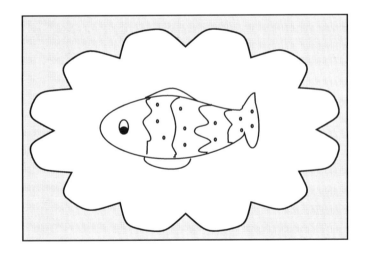

un pez

una serpiente

un conejo

un caballo

un pájaro

una tortuga

Can I say 4 animals in Spanish?

Start at "comienza aquí", roll the dice and count that number of spaces.
Say the animal you land on in Spanish. To win, arrive first at "¡Has ganado!"

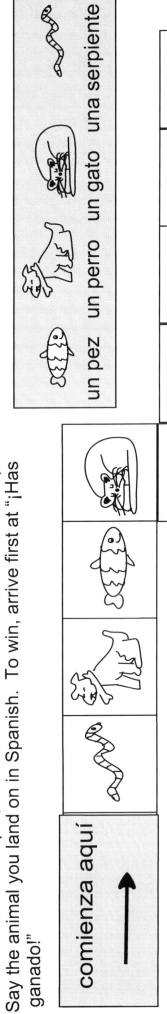

comienza aquí

un pez   un perro   un gato   una serpiente

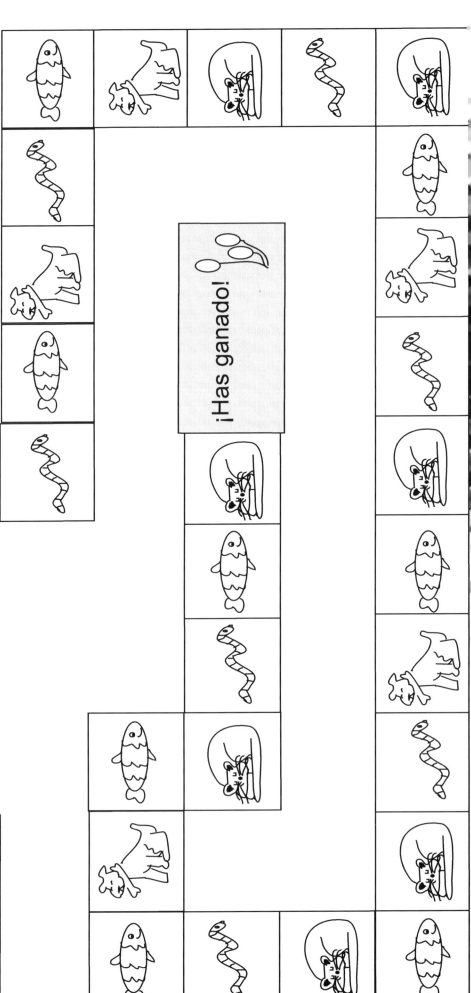

¡Has ganado!

Can I say 4 animals in Spanish?

ach person / team needs 5 coloured counters or cubes of one colour
or a set of noughts or a set of crosses).
ay the Spanish word for the animal or number as you place your counter.
o win you have to get 3 in a row (vertically, horizontally or diagonally).

un pez   un perro   un gato   una serpiente

1 = uno   2 = dos   3 = tres   4 = cuatro   5 = cinco

■ Can I say 4 animals in Spanish?

Roll two dice and find the **co-ordinate** by counting along the bottom for the first dice, and up the side for the second dice. Say the animal in Spanish for the co-ordinate to get a point, e.g. 3, 2 = un gato. The winner is the person or team who gets the most points.

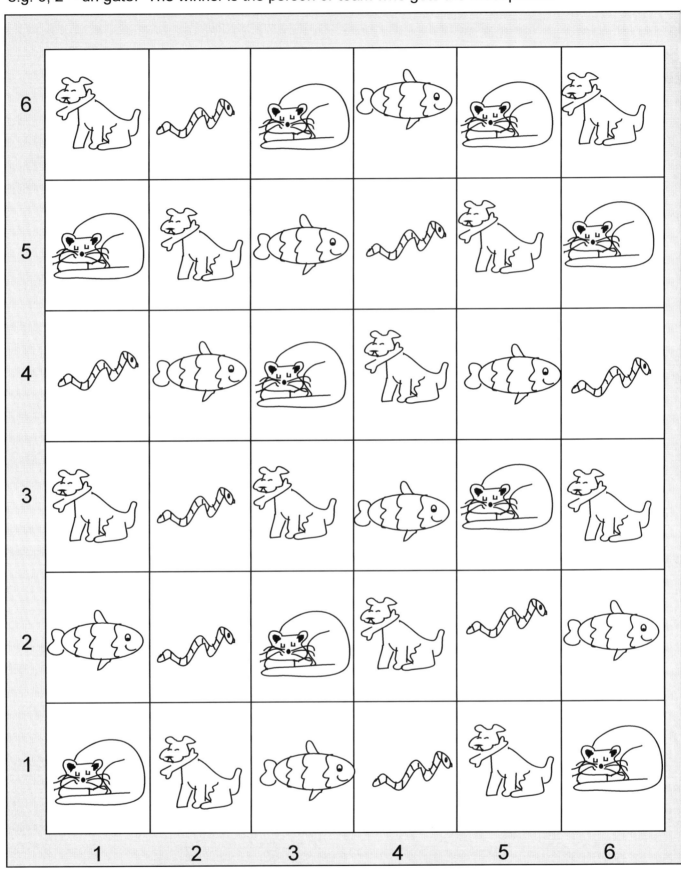

un pez   un perro   un gato   una serpiente

Can I say 6 animals in Spanish?

Start at "comienza aquí", roll the dice and count that number of squares.
Say the animal you land on in Spanish. To win, arrive first at "¡Has ganado!"

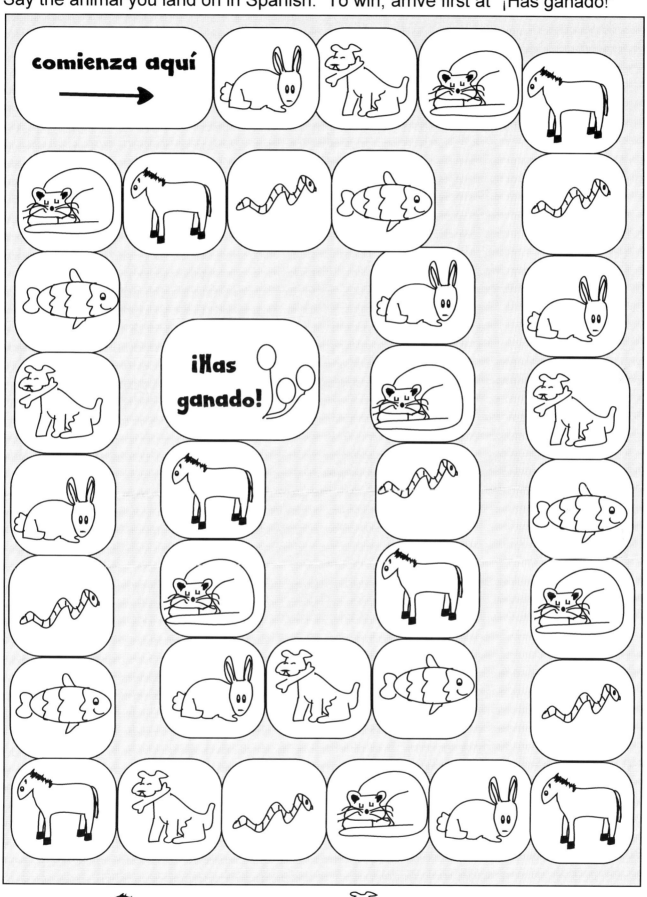

 un conejo   un caballo   un pez   un perro   un gato   una serpiente

27

■ Can I say 6 animals in Spanish?

Each person / team needs 5 coloured counters or cubes of one colour
(or a set of noughts or a set of crosses).
Say the Spanish word for the animal or number as you place your counte
To win you have to get 3 in a row (vertically, horizontally or diagonally).

2 = dos   4 = cuatro   7 = siete

un conejo   un caballo   un pez   un perro   un gato   una serpiente

Can I say 6 animals in Spanish?

Roll two dice and find the **co-ordinate** by counting along the bottom for the first dice, and up the side for the second dice. Say the animal in Spanish for the co-ordinate to get a point, e.g. 3, 2 = un gato. The winner is the person or team who gets the most points.

 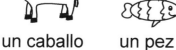

un conejo   un caballo   un pez   un perro   un gato   una serpiente

29

Can I say 9 animals in Spanish?

Each person / team needs 15 coloured counters or cubes of one colour.

Say the Spanish word for the animal as you place your counter or cube.
To win you have to get 4 in a row (vertically, horizontally or diagonally).

 un conejo   un caballo   un pez   un perro   un gato   una serpiente   un pájaro   un ratón   una tortuga

Each pupil cuts out a set of **dominoes** by cutting along the dotted lines. Take turns to put a card down by matching a word to a picture or vice versa. If you cannot match a card, miss a turn. The winner is the person to either use all their cards, or use as many cards as possible.

un pez

un conejo

un caballo

un perro

una serpiente

un gato

un ratón

un pájaro

Each pupil cuts out a set of **dominoes** by cutting along the dotted lines. Take turns to put a card down by matching a word to a picture or vice versa. If you cannot match a card, miss a turn. The winner is the person to either use all their cards, or use as many cards as possible.

 una serpiente

 un pájaro

 un perro

 un caballo

 un pez

 un gato

 una tortuga

 un conejo

Can I say 9 animals in Spanish?

Roll two dice and find the **co-ordinate** by counting along the bottom for the first dice, and up the side for the second dice. Say the animal in Spanish for the co-ordinate to get a point, e.g. 3, 2 = un gato. The winner is the person or team who gets the most points.

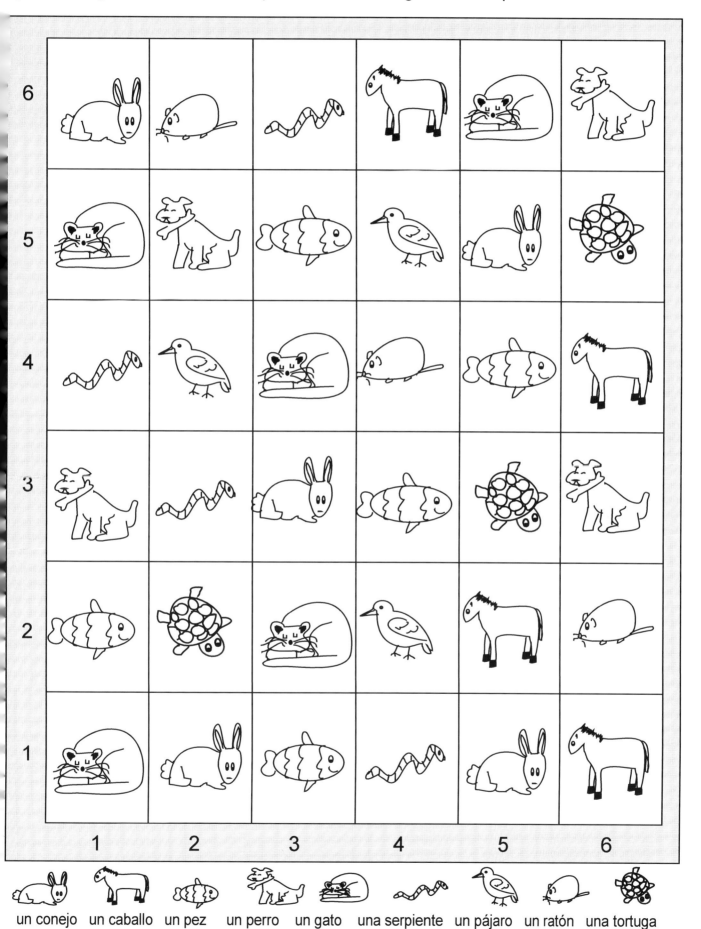

un conejo   un caballo   un pez   un perro   un gato   una serpiente   un pájaro   un ratón   una tortuga

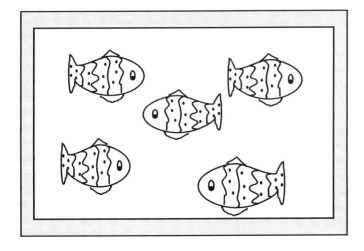

cuatro gatos	tres perros
cinco peces	**seis serpientes**
cuatro conejos	**dos caballos**
tres pájaros	**dos tortugas**

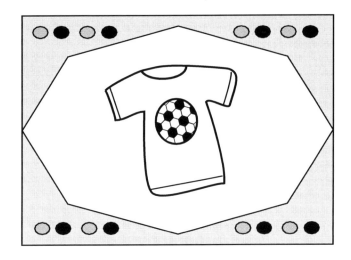

una camiseta

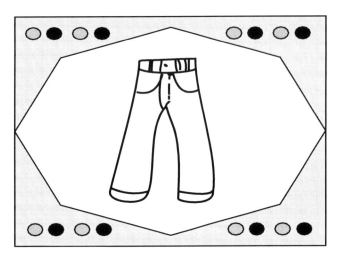

unos vaqueros

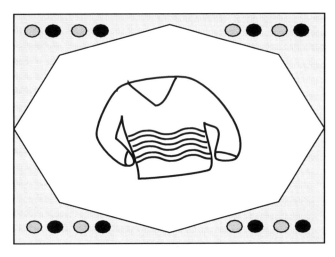

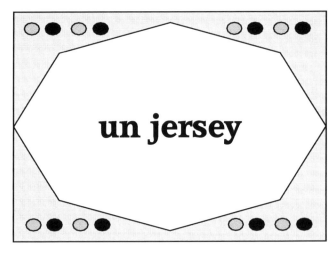

un jersey

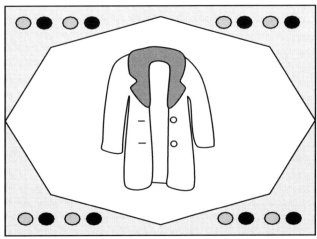

un abrigo

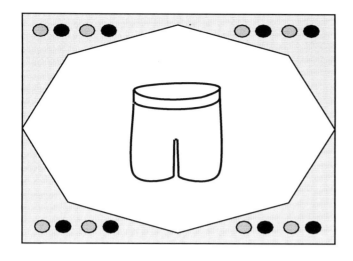

unos pantalones cortos

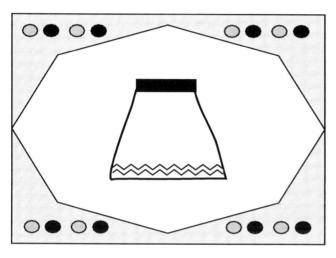

una falda

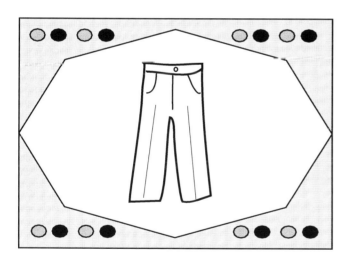

unos pantalones

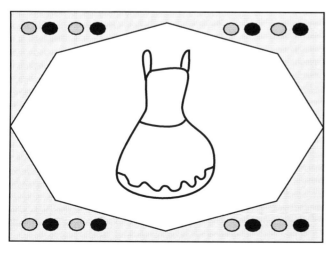

un vestido

Can I say 4 items of clothing in Spanish?

Each pupil cuts out a set of dominoes by cutting along the dotted lines. Take turns to put a card down by matching a word to a picture or vice versa. If you cannot match a card, miss a turn. The winner is the person to either use all their cards, or use as many cards as possible.

	un jersey		una camiseta
	unos vaqueros		un abrigo
	un abrigo		unos vaqueros
	una camiseta		un jersey

Can I say 4 items of clothes in Spanish? verde

Start at "Comienza aquí", roll the dice and count that number of squares. If the final square has the bottom of the ladder in it go up it, or if it has the head of a snake go down it. Say the item of clothing in the square you land on in Spanish. To win, arrive first at "¡Has ganado!"

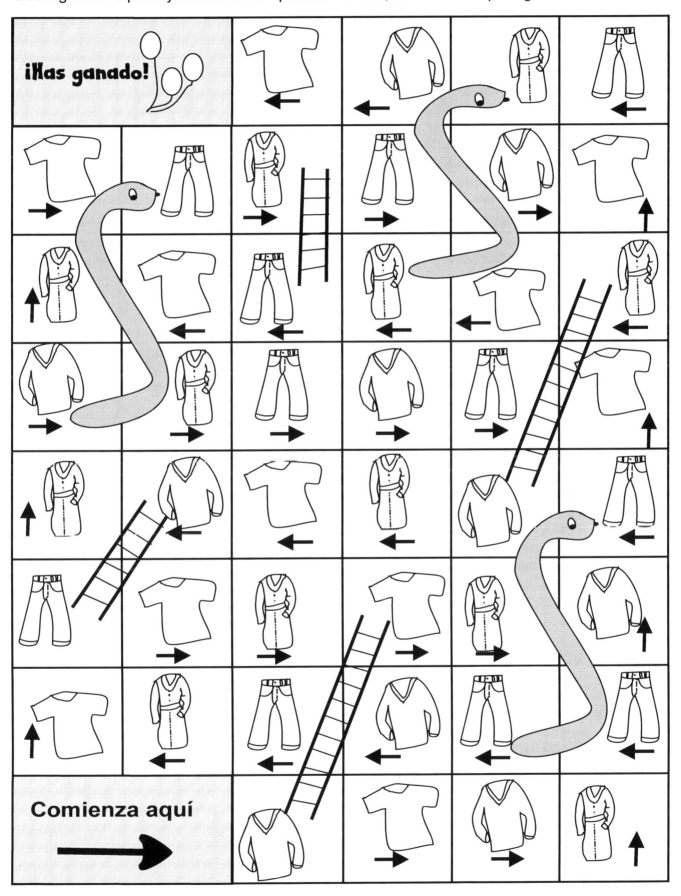

una camiseta = a t-shirt   unos vaqueros = jeans   un jersey= a jumper   un abrigo = a coat

Can I say 6 items of clothing in Spanish?

Roll the dice, and say the Spanish word for the item of clothing for the number of the dice you have thrown. Draw or write the Spanish word for the clothing if haven't got this word yet. The idea of the game is to be the first person to get all six words.

un abrigo

un jersey

una camiseta

unos vaqueros

una falda

unos pantalones cortos

40

Can I say 6 items of clothing in Spanish?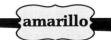

Starting at Comienza aquí, roll the dice and count that number of squares in any direction. Whatever square you land on, say and write down the Spanish word for whatever is in the square. The idea of the game is to be the first person to get all 6 items of clothes, but only write each word once.

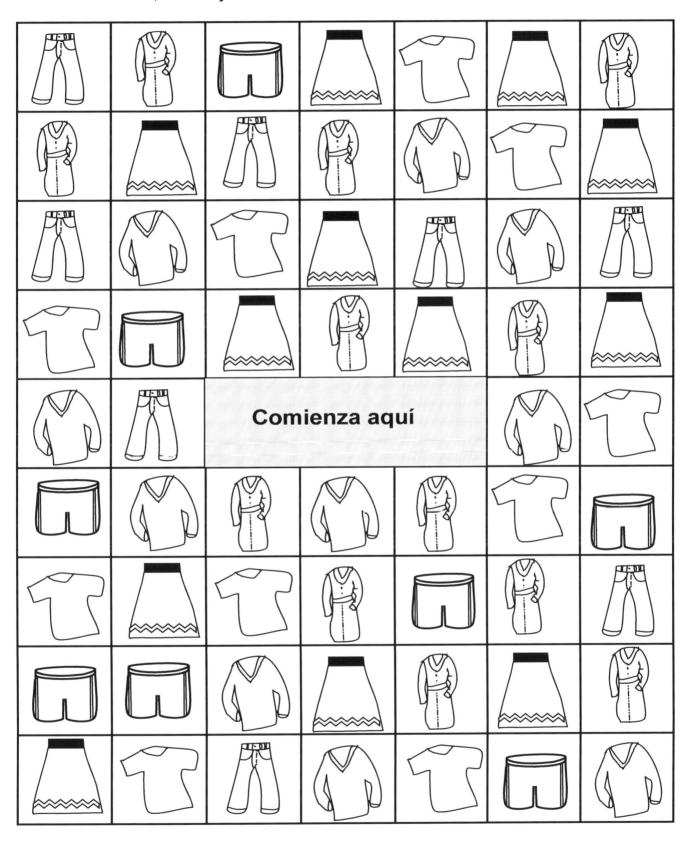

una camiseta = a t-shirt   unos vaqueros = jeans   un jersey= a jumper

un abrigo = a coat   unos pantalones cortos = shorts   una falda = a skirt

41

■ Can I say 9 items of clothing? ■ { rojo }

Each person / team needs 24 coloured counters or cubes of one colour, or can use a pencil to draw noughts or crosses directly onto the sheet. Say the Spanish word for the item of clothing as you choose a space. **To win you have to get 4 in a row** (vertically, horizontally or diagonally).

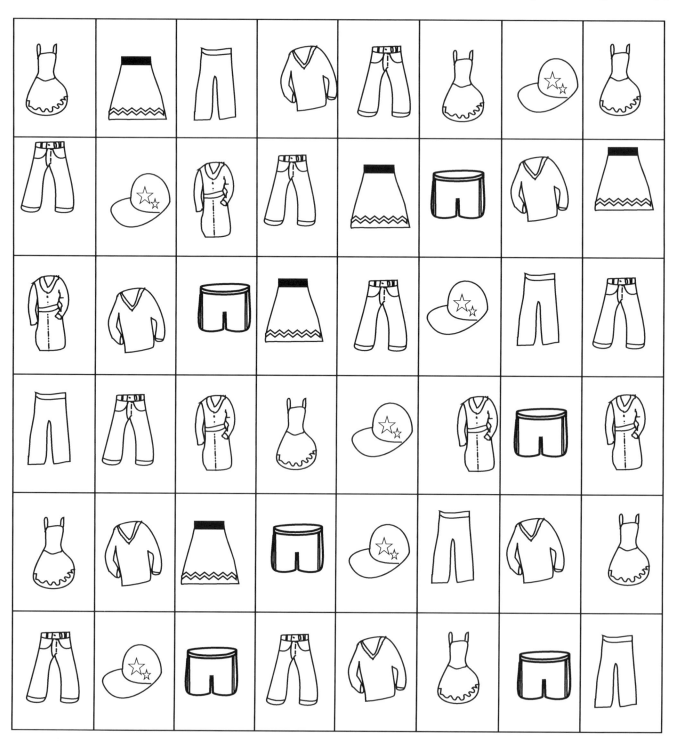

una camiseta = a t-shirt   unos vaqueros = jeans   un jersey= a jumper

un abrigo = a coat   unos pantalones cortos = shorts   una falda = a skirt

unos pantalones = trousers   una gorra = a cap   un vestido = a dress

Can I say 9 items of clothing?

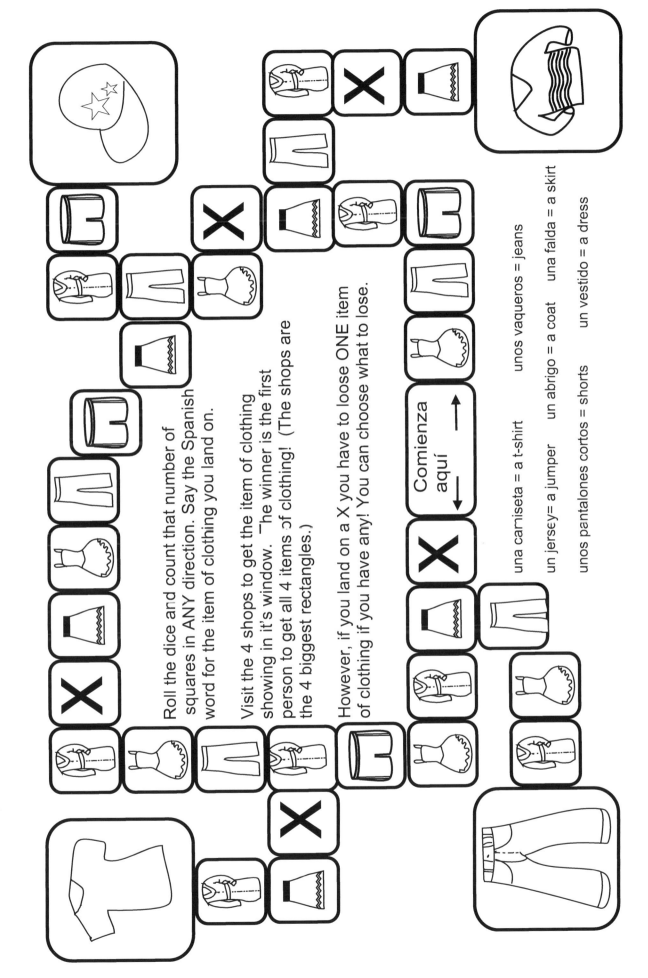

Roll the dice and count that number of squares in ANY direction. Say the Spanish word for the item of clothing you land on.

Visit the 4 shops to get the item of clothing showing in it's window. The winner is the first person to get all 4 items of clothing! (The shops are the 4 biggest rectangles.)

However, if you land on a X you have to loose ONE item of clothing if you have any! You can choose what to lose.

Comienza aquí

una camiseta = a t-shirt   unos vaqueros = jeans

un jersey= a jumper   un abrigo = a coat   una falda = a skirt

unos pantalones cortos = shorts   un vestido = a dress

el coche

el barco

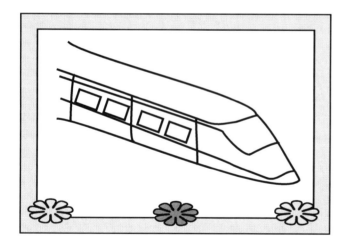

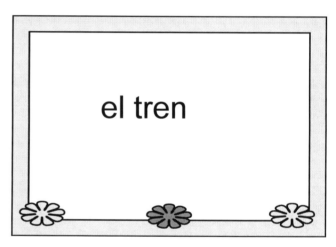

el tren

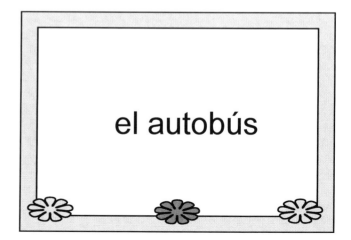

el autobús

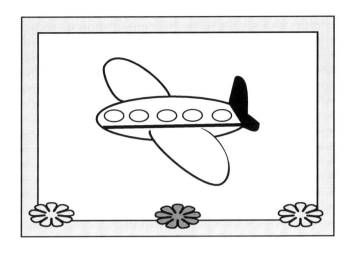

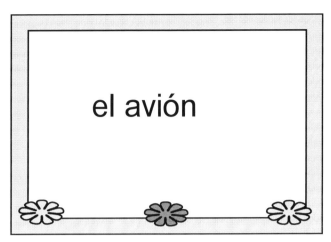

el avión

la bicicleta

la barca

la moto

Can I say 4 types of transport in Spanish?

Start at "comienza aquí", roll the dice and count that number of squares.
Say the transport you land on in Spanish. To win, arrive first at "¡Has ganado!"

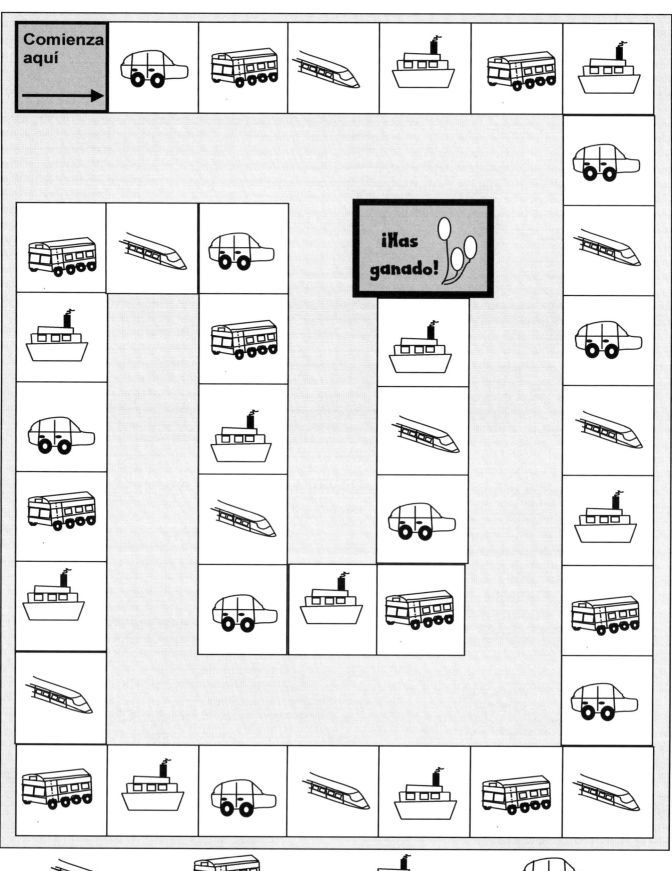

 el tren   el autobús   el barco   el coche

Can I say 4 types of transport in Spanish?

Roll two dice and find the **co-ordinate** by counting along the bottom for the first dice, and up the side for the second dice. Say the transport in Spanish for the co-ordinate to get a point, e.g. 3, 2 = el coche The winner is the person or team who gets the most points.

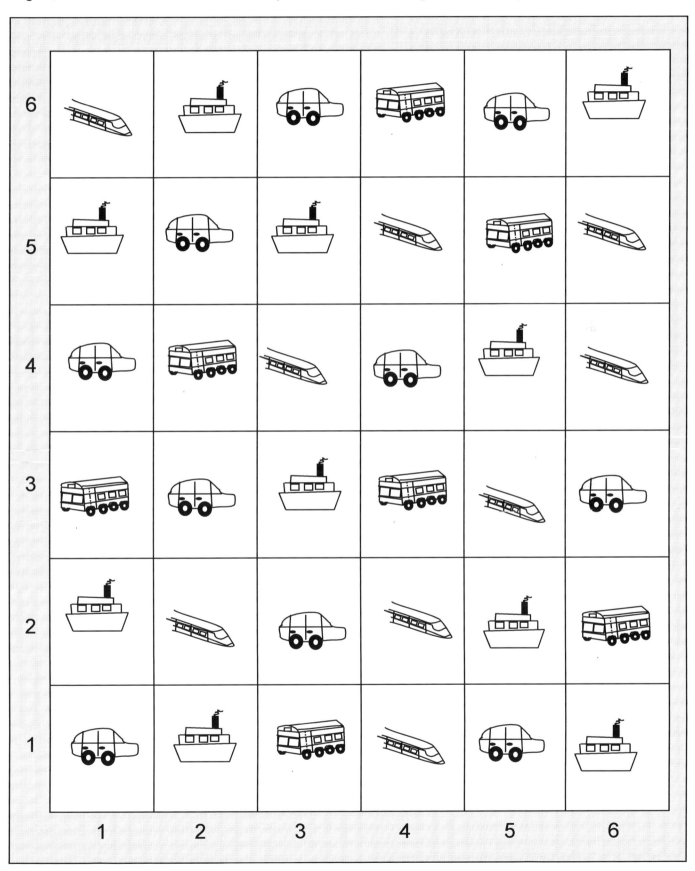

 el tren    el autobús    el barco   el coche

Can I say 6 types of transport in Spanish? amarillo

Start at "comienza aquí", roll the dice and count that number of squares.
Say the transport you land on in Spanish. To win, arrive first at "¡Has ganado!"

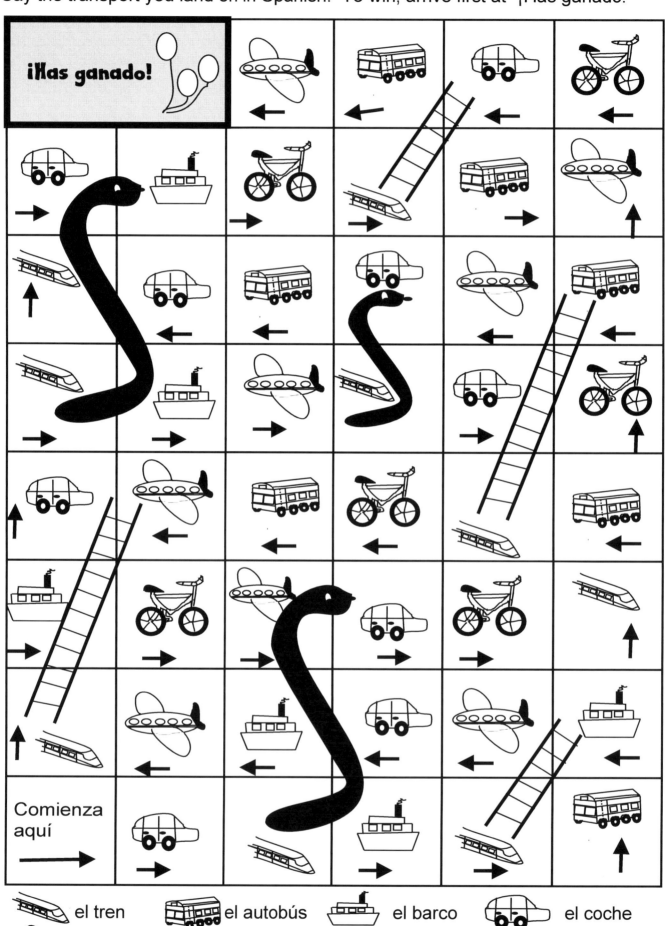

 el tren   el autobús   el barco   el coche

el avión   la bicicleta

48

Can I say 6 types of transport in Spanish? 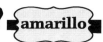 amarillo

Roll the dice, and say the Spanish word for the type of transport according to the number on the dice you have thrown.

Write the Spanish word for the type of transport or draw it's picture if haven't got this word yet.

The winner is the first person to get all six types of transport.

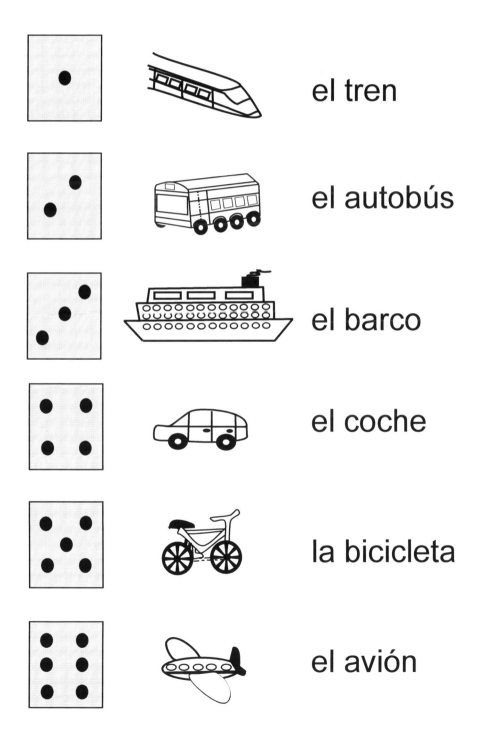

el tren

el autobús

el barco

el coche

la bicicleta

el avión

Can I say 9 types of transport in Spanish?

Start at "comienza aquí", roll the dice and count that number of squares. Say the transport you land on in Spanish.
To win, arrive first at "¡Has ganado!"

el barco
el coche
el cohete
el autobús
la moto
la bicicleta
el tren
el avión
la barca

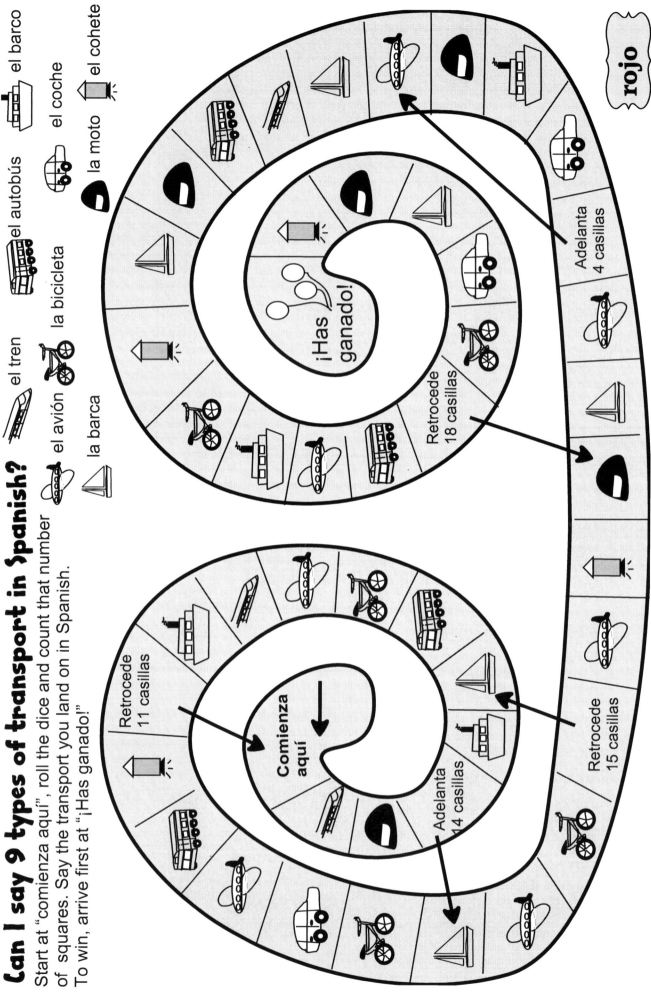

rojo

adelanta - go forward   retrocede - go back   casillas - spaces

Can I say 9 types of transport in Spanish? - Person A {rojo}

Each pupil cuts along the dotted lines to make a set of dominoes.
Take turns to put a card down by matching a word to a picture or vice versa.
If you cannot match a card, miss a turn. The winner is the person to either
use all their cards, or use as many cards as possible.

✈	el tren
🚗	el barco
(helmet)	la barca
🚲	la moto
🚌	la bicicleta
🚢	el avión
🚄	el coche
⛵	el autobús

51

Can I say 9 types of transport in Spanish? - Person B {rojo}

Each pupil cuts along the dotted lines to make a set of dominoes.
Take turns to put a card down by matching a word to a picture or vice versa.
If you cannot match a card, miss a turn. The winner is the person to either
use all their cards, or use as many cards as possible.

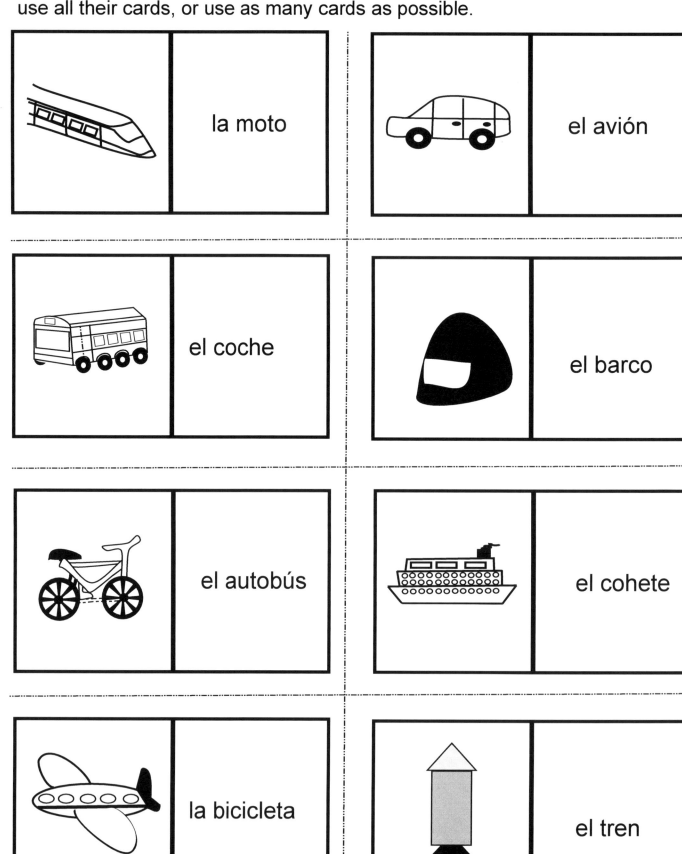

	la moto		el avión
	el coche		el barco
	el autobús		el cohete
	la bicicleta		el tren

Hace calor

Hace frío

Hace sol

Llueve

Hace buen tiempo

Hace mal tiempo

Nieva

Está nublado

54

Can I say 4 weather phrases in Spanish?

Each person / team needs 5 coloured counters or cubes of one colour (or a set of noughts or a set of crosses). Say the Spanish word for the weather or number as you place your counter.
To win you have to get 3 in a row (vertically, horizontally or diagonally).

0 °C Hace frío Llueve 30°C Hace calor 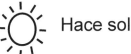 Hace sol

1 = uno   2 = dos   3= tres   4 = cuatro   5 = cinco

Can I say 4 weather phrases in Spanish?

0 °C

30°C

0 °C

30°C

30°C

0 °C

Comienza aquí

0 °C

The idea of this game is to be the first person to get 4 different Spanish weather phrases.

Start at **comienza aquí** and roll the dice. Count the number of squares shown on the dice, and say the weather phrase in Spanish for the square you land on.

Draw the picture shown for the weather phrase on a mini white board or piece of paper if you haven't yet got the phrase.

Who will be the first person to get all 4 Spanish weather phrases?

0 °C Hace frío   Llueve

30°C Hace calor   Hace sol

30°C

30°C

0 °C

30°C

0 °C

30°C

0 °C

Can I say 6 weather phrases in Spanish?

Start at "comienza aquí", roll the dice and count that number of squares.
Say the weather you land on in Spanish. To win, arrive first at "¡Has ganado!"

¡Has ganado!	☀ ←	🌧 ←	☹ ←	30°C	☀ ←
☹ →	30°C	☺ →	🌧 →	☀ →	☺ ↑
↑ 0 °C	☀ ←	0 °C	☀ ←	0 °C	30°C ←
🌧 →	30°C →	☹ →	🌧 →	☺ →	🌧 ↑
↑ ☺	☀ ←	🌧 ←	☺ ←	0 °C	☀
0 °C	🌧 →	☺ →	30°C	☀	☺ ↑
↑ ☀	30°C ←	☀ ←		☹ ←	0 °C ←
comienza aquí →	🌧 →	0 °C	30°C →	☹ →	☺ ↑

0 °C Hace frío   🌧 Llueve   **30°C** Hace calor   ☀ Hace sol   ☺ Hace buen tiempo   ☹ Hace mal tiempo

Can I say 6 weather phrases in Spanish?  amarillo

Roll two dice and find the **co-ordinate** by counting along the bottom for the first dice, and up the side for the second dice. Say the weather phrase in Spanish for the co-ordinate to get a point, e.g. 6,4 Hace Sol. The winner is the person or team who gets the most points.

	1	2	3	4	5	6
6	0 °C	☀	😊	30°C	🌧	☹
5	☹	🌧	30°C	😊	☀	0 °C
4	30°C	😊	0 °C	🌧	☹	☀
3	😊	☹	☀	0 °C	30°C	🌧
2	☀	0 °C	☹	🌧	😊	30°C
1	🌧	😊	30°C	☀	0 °C	☹

Hace buen tiempo = It's good weather   Hace sol = It's sunny   Hace calor = It's hot

Hace mal tiempo = It's bad weather   Llueve = It's raining   Hace frío = It's cold

58

Can I say 9 weather phrases in Spanish? — rojo

Start at "comienza aquí", roll the dice and count that number of squares.
Say the weather phrase you land on in Spanish. To win, arrive first at "¡Has ganado!"

adelanta - go forward   retrocede - go back   casillas - spaces

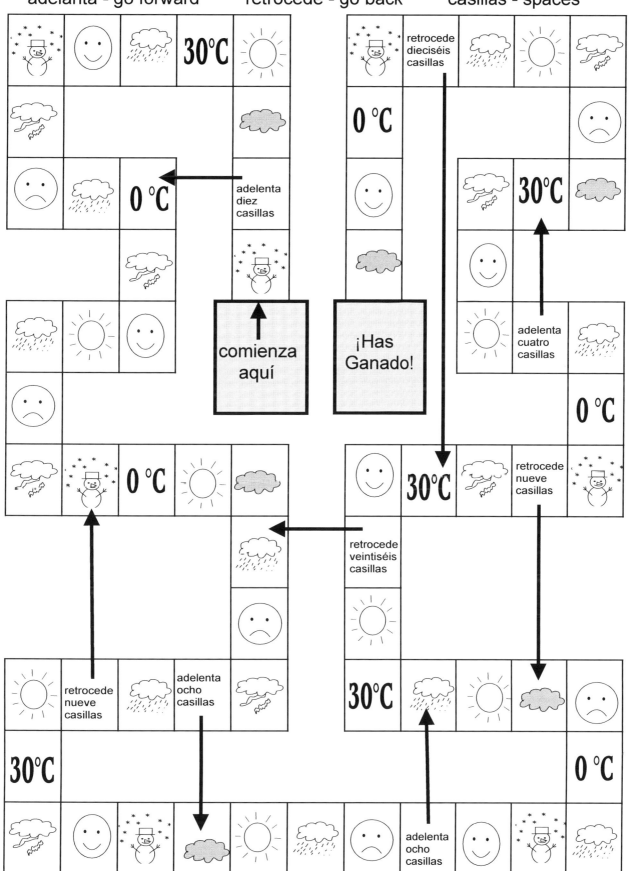

Hace buen tiempo = It's good weather   Hace sol = It's sunny   Hace calor = It's hot

Llueve = It's raining   Nieva = It's snowing   Hace mal tiempo = It's bad weather

Hace frío = It's cold   Está nublado = It's cloudy   Hay tormenta = It's stormy

Can I say 9 weather phrases in Spanish? ➡ rojo

Each person / team needs 5 coloured counters or cubes of one colour (or a set of noughts or a set of crosses). Say the Spanish word for the weather as you place your counter. To win you have to get 4 in a row (vertically, horizontally or diagonally).

☁	🌧	0 °C	☀
30°C	☺	⛄	⛈
🌧	0 °C	☺	☀
☹	⛄	⛈	⛄
☀	🌧	0 °C	☹
⛈	☁	☺	30°C
0 °C	☹	☀	☁

Hace buen tiempo = It's good weather   Hace sol = It's sunny   Hace calor = It's hot

Llueve = It's raining   Nieva = It's snowing   Hace mal tiempo = It's bad weather

Hace frío = It's cold   Está nublado = It's cloudy   Hay tormenta = It's stormy

	a	the
coke	una Coca-Cola	la Coca-Cola
lemonade	una limonada	la limonada
water	(un) agua mineral	el agua mineral
orange juice	un zumo de naranja	el zumo de naranja
diet coke	una Coca-Cola light	la Coca-Cola light
chocolate milkshake	un batido de chocolate	el batido de chocolate
tea	un té	el té
coffee	un café	el café
milk	una leche	la leche

Hola	Hello
Adiós	Goodbye
por favor	Please
gracias	Thank you
Buenos días	Good morning
Buenas tardes	Good afternoon
sí	Yes
no	No
Buenas noches	Good night
Hasta luego	Good bye
lo siento	I'm sorry
de nada	Don't mention it

un abrigo	a coat
un jersey	a jumper
una camiseta	a T-shirt
unos vaqueros	some jeans
una falda	a skirt
unos pantalones cortos	some shorts
un vestido	a dress
unos pantalones	some trousers
una gorra	a cap

61

un gato.............a cat
un perro.............a dog
un pez.............a fish
una serpiente.....a snake

un conejo.........a rabbit
un caballo........ a horse

un pájaro......... a bird
una tortuga.......a tortoise
un ratón.............a mouse

Los gatos ....cats
Los perros ....dogs
Los peces .... fishes
Las serpientes....... snakes

Los conejos ....rabbits
Los caballos...... ...horses

Los pájaros.......... birds
Las tortugas .... tortoises
Los ratones.......... mice

el tren........... the train
el autobús......the bus
el barco.........the ship
el coche........the car

el avión..........the plane
la bicicleta......the bike

la moto..........the motorbike
la barca......... the small boat
el cohete........the rocket

Hace calor....... It's hot
Hace frío........ It's cold
Hace sol.........It's sunny
Llueve.............It's raining

Hace buen tiempo...It's good
weather
Hace mal tiempo.....It's bad
weather

Nieva............. It's snowing
Hay tormenta....It's stormy
Está nublado.....It's cloudy

Ideas for games & activities using the mini cards

Parejas (Matching game / Pairs card game)

Place all the cards face down on the table. With a partner, take it in turns to find the Spanish word that matches the picture. If you find a matching pair you "win" the cards. The idea of the game is to try and find as many pairs as possible. Say the Spanish words for the cards as you turn over the cards.

¿Qué carta es? (Guess the card)

In pairs, each person takes a card. Make sure your partner does not see your card! Take turns to guess each other's card. If you guess the card correctly, you "win" the card.

You should both then take another card for your partner to guess. The winner is the person who wins the most cards.

¿Cómo dicen las palabras? (How do you say the words?)

Put all the cards together in a pile, and shuffle the cards. Take it in turns with a partner to take a card:
If it is a picture card, say the Spanish word for the card.
If it is an Spanish word, say what it means in English.

If you know the word you "win" the card. If you don't know the word put the card in a separate pile and at the end of the game check what it means. The idea of the game is to win as many cards as possible.

¿Qué falta? (Which one is missing?)

Put all the picture cards face up on the table. Pupil A closes their eyes and pupil B takes away one card. Pupil A has to say which card is missing in Spanish. Then swap roles.

Note to teachers: For the mini card activities you can either give the pupils all the cards or you can differentiate the activities as outlined on page 1.

Fui al mercado y compré ....

(I went to the market and bought.....)

In pairs, take it in turns to say **Hay** (there is), then add a card of your own choice and place this card face down on the table.

The next person has to repeat **Hay** and the previous card or cards that were said before saying **y** (and) and then their choice of word, and placing this word also face down next to the previous card or cards.

Try not to look at the cards that are face down on the table unless you need to check the word after it has been said.

E.g. Person A :   Hay un coche
     Person B :   Hay un coche y un tren
     Person A :   Hay un coche, un tren y un barco

¿Cuál es la palabra española? (What Spanish word is it?)

In pairs, pupil A takes a card and draws a picture for this word on their partner's back. Pupil B has to guess in Spanish the word in order to win the card. Then the pupils swap roles.

This game can also be used for practising numbers. To practice numbers draw a number as a figure on each other's back, and say the number in Spanish.

¿Es masculino o femenino? (Is it masculine or feminine?)

Using the mini cards, arrange the cards according to if the words are masculine (boy words) or feminine (girl words).

Masculine words start with either **un** (a) or **el** (the) or **los** (the plural)

Feminine words start with either **una** (a) or **la** (the) or **las** (the plural)

¡Bebamos algo! (Lets have a drink!)

Half of the class are waiters or waitresses and have the mini cards for the drinks .

The other half of the class are customers. Waiters and waitresses go to the customers who are seated around the room. Customers can only order one thing from each waiter or waitress, but can be served by various waiters or waitresses. Customers receive the mini card for what they order.

Customers can ask for the card by adding **por favor** (please) after the Spanish word for what they order or by saying **Me gustaría………por favor** (I would like ……please).

Note to teachers: If the mini cards are being handed out to the customers, you may need several sets of cards per waiter / waitress or you can give some blank cards for any extra cards the pupils need.

Mimo (Mimes)

For the animals, transport and weather topics: In pairs, take it in turns to take a card and then do a mime to your partner so they can guess in Spanish what the word is.

If the card is guessed correctly, turn the card upwards in front of you. See how many cards you can win!

Muéstrame..... (Show me....)

In table groups, or as a whole class everyone has a set of cards each.

The teacher or a pupil says one of the Spanish words.
Challenge everyone to be the first to hold up the correct card.

Note to teachers:
If you are playing this game with the whole class you can differentiate this activity by giving the pupils the cards for the suggested key words for their group (verde, amarillo, rojo) as shown at the front of this book. Then, before you say Muestrame…., you could tell the class if this time it's for los verdes/ los amarillos / los rojos.

Las opiniones (opinions)

Using the mini cards, work with a partner to say if you like or dislike the thing pictured:

Me gusta / Me gustan ………………… I like

No me gusta / No me gustan…………. I don't like

¿y a ti?……….. And you?

Me gusta / No me gusta is used when the word that follows is in the singular.
Me gustan / No me gustan is used when the word that follows is in the plural.
E.g. Me gusta la Coca-Cola.   Me gustan los gatos.

Pareja de cartas (snap)

Divide the cards equally between 2 people. Take turns to say the Spanish word for the card as you place the card face up on the table.

You will need to make a pile of cards each so that you can see if two cards are the same. If the two top cards are the same, to win both piles of cards you have to be the first person to say the Spanish word for the top card as you place your hand down on the pile of cards.

Note to teachers: pupils ideally have a minimum of 4 cards for each word being practiced.

El campeonato (the championship)

Working as a class or in table groups, two pupils compete at the same time to translate the word first from Spanish to English, or vice versa. The two pupils who are competing stand up by their chair, and they do not need to put up their hand to answer as they can just call out the answer.
One person has the mini cards and says whatever is on the top card. Whoever says the word first out of the two competitors stays on, and a new pupil then stands on to take on the winner.

Encuentra la pareja (Find the matching card)

This game can use either just one topic (but have several cards for each word so there are enough cards for the whole class or group) or can be used as revision for various topics.

Divide the cards so everyone has one card. The idea of the game is to find the matching picture card for the Spanish word card, and vice versa. To do this, walk round the room saying your Spanish word until you find a matching card.

Once you have found a match you could either get a new card from the teacher, or you could be asked to sit down and draw and label your word on a mini whiteboard.

¿Recuerdas dónde están las cartas?
(Do you remember where the cards are?)

Look at the cards and say the Spanish words for the mini cards as you place them face down on the table. When all the cards are on the table take turns to see who can identify correctly the Spanish word before you turn over a card.

Who can win the most cards?

Actividad escrita (Written activity)

Using one of the phrases from the next section in the book, write a piece of work by randomly choosing a mini card and then write the corresponding sentence.

(If any of the mini cards appear twice, you do not need to do the sentence again.)

Suggestions for making sentences using the games

To develop the formation of sentences and questions, once the pupils are familiar with the words for a particular topic, teach one group or the whole class one of the phrases below and ask them to play the game using this phrase before they say the words that are pictured in the games. The pupils could write the phrase being practised on a mini whiteboard in front of them, or you could write the phrase on the IWB on whiteboard in the classroom.

Drinks

1) **Asking for a drink: Me gustaría tomar…… por favor** (I would like …….please)
e.g. Me gustaría tomar un zumo de naranja, por favor.
Or say the drink, and then por favor after it e.g. una Coca-Cola, por favor.

2) **Saying what you are drinking**: Bebo (I am drinking) e.g. Bebo una limonada.

3) **Giving opinions or preferences about drinks:**

Me gusta = I like   No me gusta = I don't like   Prefiero = I prefer

Tell the pupils that when they say what drinks they like, dislike or prefer they need To use either el or la (the) instead of the un or una (a).

4) **Asking what drink friends like:** Te gusta……….? (Do you like…….?)
e.g. ¿Te gusta el café?

5) **Saying what is healthy to drink:**
Es bueno para la salud beber …… (It's good for your health to drink…..)
e.g. Es bueno para la salud beber agua.

Es malo para la salud beber…(It's bad for your health to drink….)
e.g. Es malo para la salud beber Coca-Cola.

6) **Saying there isn't certain drinks** (as unfortunately sometimes cafés run out or may not sell what you want).
No hay….. (There isn't)   e.g. No hay Coca-Cola light.

Greetings

Greeting people: Explain to the pupils that **señor** is used to for a man or a boy, **señora** for a woman and **señorita** is used for a girl. The pupils can play the games and say a variety of señor, señora or señorita after the greetings.

You can also introduce the word **amigo** (friend) to be used after the greetings. Amigo is used for one male friend, amiga for one female friend. In the plural, an s is added to the end.

Pet animals

1) **Saying if you have a pet**:   Tengo = I have   e.g. Tengo un gato

2) **Asking a friend if they have a particular animal:** ¿Tienes…..? (Do you have…?)
E.g. ¿Tienes un perro?   ¿Tienes un conejo?

3) **Describing the colour of the animals:** Ask the pupils to invent a colour for each
of the pets, and say the colour after the Spanish word for the animal. The games can
be coloured in by the pupils. e.g. un perro negro,   un conejo gris.

For una tortuga or una serpiente, some of the endings of the colours change as
they are both feminine nouns. The colours ending in o change the o to a after a
feminine noun in the singular: e.g. una serpiente roja, una tortuga negra.

4) **Is it big or small?**: Ask the pupils to decide if the animal is big or small,
and say either grande (big) or pequeño (small) after the Spanish word for the animal.
Explain that for una tortuga and una serpiente pequeño changes to pequeña.
e.g. un gato pequeño,   una tortuga pequeña

5) **Saying if you would like a particular animal**:

Me gustaría….(I would like …..) e.g. Me gustaría un pájaro, Me gustaría un caballo

No me gustaría …. (I wouldn't like…) e.g. No me gustaría una serpiente.

6) **Saying that you used to have a particular animal:** Tenía… (I used to have…)
e.g. Tenía un pez,   Tenía una tortuga

7) **Talking about which pets you like**: Tell the pupils that for saying if they like a
particular animal they need to say the Spanish for "I like" in the plural and also the type
of animal they like. There is a photocopiable list of the animals in the plural in the
word list section.

Me gustan = I like (plural)   e.g. Me gustan los gatos

No me gustan = I don't like (plural)   e.g. No me gustan los perros

8) **Saying which animals you prefer:** Prefiero….. (I prefer).
For saying which animal you prefer you need to say the animals in the plural:
E.g. Prefiero los gatos.

9) **Saying if you have several pets**:
Tengo = I have e.g. Tengo cinco perros, Tengo tres gatos…..
Ask the pupils to change un or una to another number and to pretend they have this
amount of the animals pictured.

Clothes

1) **Saying what you wear / are wearing:**
Llevo = I wear / I am wearing   e.g. Llevo unos vaqueros y una camiseta.
This can be extended by starting the sentence with either en verano (in summer)
or en invierno (in winter) e.g. En invierno, llevo un abrigo.
It can also be extended by talking about what you wear for school, or what you
are wear for a party.   Para ir a la escuela, llevo….. (To go to school, I wear)
Para ir a una fiesta, llevo…..(To go to a party, I wear)

2) **Saying what someone else (he /she) wears / is wearing:**
Lleva = he/she wears / is wearing
e.g..Lleva un vestido

3) **Asking a friend what they are wearing:**
¿Llevas……? (Are you wearing….?)
e.g. ¿Llevas un abrigo?

4) **Going shopping**: Pupils ask for the item by saying Me gustaría …… por favor.
(I would like…… please) e.g. Me gustaría una camiseta, por favor.
Or alternatively, just say the item of clothing, then add por favor (please).
e.g. Unos vaqueros, por favor.

5) **Describing the colour of the clothes**: Pupils either invent a colour for the item
of clothing, or colour in the games. Tell the pupils to say first the item of clothing,
then the colour e.g. un jersey azul.

Explain that for feminine words (una falda, una camiseta, una gorra….)
The colour endings may change:
rojo > roja   blanco > blanca   negro > negra   amarillo > amarilla

The following stay the same after feminine singular nouns:
azul, verde, marrón, naranja, rosa, gris, lila

For masculine plural nouns (unos pantalones cortos, unos vaqueros,
unos pantalones) the colours are as follows:
rojos, blancos, negros, amarillos, azules, verdes, marrones, naranjas,
rosas, grises, lilas

If you decide to not introduce all the rules regarding colour endings, you can choose
some colours for the pupils to choose from the colours that are the same for both
masculine and feminine nouns in the singular, and just teach the plural.
For example, you could just teach that the following colours change for the shorts,
jeans and trousers:
azul > azules   verde > verdes   lila > lilas

Transport

1) **Going shopping**: Pupils ask for a toy version of the transport by saying
Me gustaría……por favor. (I would like…..please).
e.g. Me gustaría un tren, por favor.
Or alternatively, just say the transport word, then add por favor (please).
e.g. Un coche, por favor.

2) **Describing the colour of the transport**: Pupils invent a colour for the item of transport, saying first the item of transport then the colour. e.g. un avión amarillo. Explain that for **feminine words** (una bicicleta) the colour endings may change:
e.g. una bicicleta negra.

Some colours change the **o** to an **a** for feminine words in the singular:

rojo > roja   blanco > blanca   negro > negra   amarillo > amarilla

If you decide to not introduce the fact that some endings of colours change, you can instruct the pupils to decide if the item of transport is one of the colours that don't change when the word is feminine. The games can be coloured in by the pupils.

3) **Talking about how you like to travel**: Me gusta viajar en (I like to travel by)
e.g. Me gusta viajar en tren (I like to travel by train).

4) **Talking about how you travel on holiday**:
Cuando voy de vacaciones, voy en …….(When I go on holiday I go by…..)
e.g. Cuando voy de vacaciones, voy en avión.

Este año voy en.. … (This year I go by…)
e.g. Este año voy en tren.

Weather

1) **Saying what the weather is like for certain months:**
en abril (in April)   en agosto (in August)   en diciembre (in December)
e.g. En abril llueve.   En agosto hace sol.   En diciembre nieva.

2) **Saying what the weather is like for certain days of the week:**
el lunes (on Monday)   el martes (on Tuesday)   el miércoles (on Wednesday)
el jueves (on Thursday) el viernes (on Friday)   el sábado (on Saturday)
el domingo (on Sunday).

3) **Saying what clothes you wear according to what the weather is:**
Cuando………., llevo……….. (When ………, I wear…….)
e.g. Cuando hace frío, llevo un abrigo.

Design your own board game!

In each space draw something to represent a word or write a word. To play, start at "comienza aquí", roll the dice & count that number of spaces. Say the word you land on in Spanish. To win, arrive first at "¡Has ganado!"

¡Has ganado!

comienza aquí

For children aged 7 - 11 there are the following books by Joanne Leyland:

Italian
Cool Kids Speak Italian (books 1, 2 & 3)
On Holiday in Italy Cool Kids Speak Italian
Photocopiable Games For Teaching Italian
Stories: Un Alieno Sulla Terra, La Scimmia Che Cambia Colore, Hai Un Animale Domestico?

French
Cool Kids Speak French (books 1 & 2)
Cool Kids Speak French - Special Christmas Edition
On Holiday in France Cool Kids Speak French
Photocopiable Games For Teaching French
Cool Kids Do Maths In French
Stories: Un Alien Sur La Terre, Le Singe Qui Change De Couleur, Tu As Un Animal?

Spanish
Cool Kids Speak Spanish (books 1, 2 & 3)
Cool Kids Speak Spanish - Special Christmas Edition
On Holiday in Spain Cool Kids Speak Spanish
Photocopiable Games For Teaching Spanish
Cool Kids Do Maths In Spanish
Stories: Un Extraterrestre En La Tierra, El Mono Que Cambia De Color, Seis Mascotas Maravillosas

German
Cool Kids Speak German books 1 & 2
Cool Kids Speak German book 3 (coming soon)

English as a foreign language
Cool Kids Speak English books 1 & 2

For children aged 5 - 7 there are the following books by Joanne Leyland:

French
Young Cool Kids Learn French
Sophie And The French Magician
Daniel And The French Robot (books 1, 2 & 3)
Daniel And The French Robot Teacher's Resource Book (coming soon)
Jack And The French Languasaurus (books 1, 2 & 3)

German
Young Cool Kids Learn German

Spanish
Young Cool Kids Learn Spanish
Sophie And The Spanish Magician
Daniel And The Spanish Robot (books 1, 2 & 3)
Daniel And The Spanish Robot Teacher's Resource Book (coming soon)
Jack And The Spanish Languasaurus (books 1, 2 & 3)

For more information on the books available, and different ways of learning a foreign language go to **www.foreignlanguagesforchildren.com**

Printed in Great Britain
by Amazon